Special Dedication

To John Maxwell for mentoring me concerning the concepts of teaching biblical stewardship to the local church. John, it's been quite a journey since 1973 when we designed our first stewardship campaign, "Stewards Together," in Lancaster, Ohio. Thanks for letting me preach the third sermon of the series, "Stewardship of Time." It changed my life and caused me to emphasize stewardship for a full month once a year in my local churches. You are the foremost authority on biblical stewardship in the church world.

STEWARDSHIP
STARTERS

An Instruction Book on Giving for Pastors and Lay Leaders

Stan Toler

FOREWORD

The purpose of this book is to assist pastors and lay leaders in sharing the most basic biblical principles of Christian stewardship. In an age of Xers, busters, boomers, and builders, it is the rare person who can effectively communicate across these significant generational boundaries.

Stan Toler has successfully brought together an entire assemblage of useful stewardship quotes, meditations, humorous stories, scripture, and strategic planning ideas. Use these materials wisely, and a significant deepening of commitment to biblical stewardship principles will most certainly be the result.

Steve Weber
Director
Stewardship Development Ministries
Church of the Nazarene

INTRODUCTION

According to Webster, a steward is a person who manages the affairs of a household as an estate for the owner. In a biblical sense, a steward is a manager of God's affairs on planet earth.

Recently, I have become alarmed over giving patterns in the local church. George Barna has revealed that church giving continues to decline and is extremely low among baby boomers and baby busters. Win Arn has said, "The average senior gives seven times more per week than a Baby Boomer or Buster attending the same church!" If that is true, God help us if our seniors leave us too suddenly!

The Protestant Reformation led by Martin Luther was sparked primarily because of attitudes toward money. It is my prayer that church leaders will take the principles from this book and apply them widely in the local church. My prayer is for a renewal of biblical stewardship in churches everywhere.

Stan Toler
Ephesians 3:20-21

A Prayer of Those Who Care

I do not know how long I'll live;
But while I live, Lord, let me give
Some comfort to someone in need
By smile or nod—kind word or deed,
And let me do whate'er I can
To ease things for my fellow man.
I want naught but to do my part,
to lift a tired or weary heart—
To change folks' frowns to smiles again
Then I will not have lived in vain,
And I'll not care how long I'll live
If I can give—and give—and give!

—Anonymous

STEWARDSHIP SEEDS

Quotes and insights from leaders

❀ God demands our tithes and deserves our offerings.

Stephen Olford

❀ We make a living through what we get; we make a life through what we give.

Winston Churchill

❀ He who waits to do a great deal of good all at once will never do anything.

Samuel Johnson

Giving protects us from selfishness.
Giving ensures that our needs will
be met.
Giving reminds us that we are stewards
of all we have. (1 Timothy 6:17-18)

Dan Reiland

❦ You can't fake stewardship. Your checkbook reveals all that you really believe about stewardship. A lifestyle could be written from a checkbook.

Ron Blue

❦ If God is your partner, make your plans big!

D. L. Moody

❦ Giving satisfies the soul, edifies the church, and magnifies the Lord.

Stephen Olford

The world asks, what does a man own?
Christ asks, how does he use it?
The world thinks more
about the money getting;
Christ, about the money giving.
And when a man gives,
the world still asks, what does he give?
Christ asks, how does he give?

Andrew Murray

God has given us two hands—one to receive with and the other to give with. We are not cisterns made for hoarding; we are channels made for sharing.

Billy Graham

It pays to serve God, but it doesn't pay to serve God because it pays.

R. G. LeTourneau

Make money your god and it will plague you like the devil!

Henry Fielding

Some say, dedicate the heart
and the money will follow;
but our Lord put it the other way around.
"Where your treasure is,
there will your heart be also."

G. Timothy Johnson

The only safe rule is to give more than we can spare.

C. S. Lewis

The gift of 10% has precedence all the way back to the time of Abraham. Tithing is a guide to giving for today's Christian.

Wayne Watts

I will place no value on anything I may possess except in relation to the kingdom of Christ. I will use my possessions to promote the glory of Him to whom I owe all.

David Livingstone

I have watched 100,000 families over my years of investment counseling. I always saw greater prosperity and happiness among those families who tithed than among those who didn't. Tithing is simply an outward expression of spiritual growth, and spiritual growth leads to material growth.

Sir John Templeton

❦ When it comes to giving, some folks will stop at nothing!

Jimmy Carter

❦ Make all you can, save all you can, give all you can!

John Wesley

❦ There never was a person who did anything worth doing who did not receive more than he gave.

Henry Ward Beecher

To effectively lead, you must be able to raise . . .

> . . . morale
> . . . leaders
> . . . money.

John Maxwell

❦ Generous giving is the result of an inspired motive.
Melvin McCullough

❦ The most important aspect of tithing and stewardship is not the raising of money for the church, but the development of devoted Christians.
Fred M. Wood

❦ Good stewardship acknowledges the absolute and ultimate claims of God.
Frank Stagg

Motive tells us something about how we give.
Purpose tells something about why we give.

James E. Carter

❀ Gifted believers are accountable to God for the stewardship of their time, talent, and tithe.

Doug Carter

❀ Stewardship involves more than money. It involves the commitment of your time, your health, and the sharing of the Gospel.

John Maxwell

❀ God gives to us what He knows will flow through us.

Robert Schuller

I do not believe one can settle how much we ought to give.
I am afraid the only safe rule is to give more than we can spare.

C. S. Lewis

A philosopher has been defined as one who cannot enjoy life for wondering about it. Often it is that way with Christian stewardship. Many people spend their faith regarding it, limp in the methods of fulfilling its demands, and spend their time speculating as to its meaning.

J. B. Chapman

Christian stewardship is more than the management of things; it is the refusal to let things manage us.

James A. Lollis

❀ I know God will not give me anything I can't handle. I just wish that he didn't trust me so much.

Mother Teresa

❀ The dead take to the grave,
clutched in their hands,
only what they have given away.

DeWitt Wallace

❦ Giving to the church is the last thing to arrive and the first thing to go . . .

Conrad Lowe

❦ There are three conversions necessary: the conversion of the heart, mind, and the purse.

Martin Luther

❦ The greatness of a church is determined not by what it takes in, but by what it sends out.

Talmadge Johnson

It is one of the most beautiful compensations in life that one cannot sincerely try to help another without helping himself.

Ralph Waldo Emerson

❦ If the church has a need, God has pre-arranged supply to meet that need through His people.

Terry N. Toler

❦ All of life involves stewardship—tithing is the best way to acknowledge that God owns all I possess.

Frank Broyles

❦ Stewardship is what a man does after he says, "I believe."

W. H. Greever

Tithing contributes to spiritual growth and maturity. Tithe, and we will have solid food upon which to nourish our souls.

David F. Nixon

❀ To be able to live a spiritual life in the midst of a materialistic environment has been and is the perpetual problem of religion.

E. Stanley Jones

❀ Informed givers are happy givers!

Stan Toler

❀ Stewardship is inclusive—it includes every aspect of life.

T. B. Matson

Recognition of God's ownership of all things and man's stewardship responsibility.

Decision to put God's will first in life and possessions.

Dedication of time, talents and money to the purpose of God in the world.

Dedication to give regularly, abundantly and cheerfully to the work of God through His church. The tithe is the Lord's (Lev. 27:30). The Christian who makes a tithing commitment gives witness to his faith in Christ.

Arthur Davenport

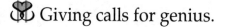 Stewardship is the acceptance from God of personal responsibility for all of life and life's offerings.

R. T. Williams

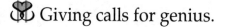 To give away money is an easy matter and is in any man's power. But to decide to whom to give it and how large and when and for what purpose is neither in every man's power nor an easy matter. Hence it is that such excellence is rare, praiseworthy and noble.

Aristotle

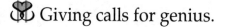 Giving calls for genius.

Ovid

A man's life is not determined
by its duration,
but by its distinctives.

Howard Hendricks

STEWARDSHIP STEPS

*Strategic steps
to help churches increase
their weekly
tithes and offerings*

❀ Plan your offering time each Sunday.

❀ Use innovative ideas to raise your weekly income.
- humor
- scriptures
- brief stories
- testimonials

❀ Model the spirit of giving from the pulpit. When you ask for a dollar, give a dollar!

❀ Plan a full month of stewardship emphasis once a year.

Tips for Stewardship Month

- Form a stewardship ministry action team
- Select a theme
- Send out weekly letters
- Distribute the annual church budget on the Sunday you speak on giving
- Preach a series of sermons on stewardship
- Ask for a commitment

❦ Inform your congregation of significant offering achievements.

❦ Praise your congregation for their faithfulness in giving.

❦ Spend time with your top givers.

☘ Teach new Christians biblical steward-ship concepts. It will help them . . .

- discover their spiritual gifts
- increase their level of commitment to God
- experience beautiful blessings
- impact a lost world for Christ

❀ Distribute numbered tithing envelopes to all church attenders. It will stimulate giving and enhance record-keeping.

❀ Mail quarterly giving statements to all parishioners. Two things will happen immediately:

- You will be able to reconcile incorrect records
- You will see an increase in giving the next Sunday

❧ Never "take" the offering. Rather, "receive" the offering. Make offering time a time of celebration!

❧ Teach the twofold biblical basis for giving to the entire congregation:
- God owns all things (Lev. 25:23)
- God owns us (Rom. 14:8)

❦ Teach children the importance of giving. Always include them in building campaigns and world mission offering opportunities.

❦ Never ask for money at events that have been designed to reach the unchurched.

❦ Encourage potential givers to form a partnership with God.

❧ Appeal to the six pockets of giving:
- maintenance pocket
- missions pocket
- benevolence pocket
- buildings pocket
- education pocket
- evangelism pocket

If you don't use a pocket, you lose it!

❦ Emphasize giving as an act of worship.

❦ Offer workshops on money management and financial planning.

❦ Always celebrate the generosity of God's people.

❀ Share Waldo Werning's three levels of giving:
- you have to (law)
- you ought to (obligation)
- you want to (grace)

✂ Preach on the Macedonian Models of Giving (2 Cor. 8:1-9):
- They gave willingly.
- They gave beyond their ability.
- They gave enthusiastically.
- They gave their best.

❦ Plan a biblically based financial campaign for your new building. Always include the following ingredients:

- Prayerful planning
- God's timing
- Organization and training
- Enthusiastic promotion
- Vision communication

❧ Communicate the fourfold aspects of biblical stewardship:

1. Stewardship of life
2. Stewardship of relationships
3. Stewardship of the gospel
4. Stewardship of time, spiritual gifts, and money

STEWARDSHIP STORIES

Humor in the pulpit

❦ New offering plate for churches:
This ingenious invention receives gifts of a dollar or more on a plush cushion with silent graciousness. But when half-dollars are dropped in, it rings a bell; when quarters are given, it blows a whistle; when dimes are slipped in, it fires a shot. But when someone refuses to give, it takes their picture.

Perhaps you've heard about the circus athlete who earned his living by displaying astonishing feats of physical strength. His show would normally conclude with a simple, but impressive, demonstration of his ability to squeeze an orange dry. After completing his act, he would then challenge the audience to produce anyone who could extract even one drop of juice from the crushed orange.

On one of these occasions a little man volunteered. He was so diminutive that his very appearance raised a laugh from the spectators. Undaunted, however, the man stepped onto the stage and took from the athlete what appeared to be nothing more than a shriveled up piece of rind. Then, bracing himself, he slowly and firmly compressed his right hand. Every eye was on him, and the atmosphere was electric. A moment or two elapsed, and then, to everyone's amazement—and not least the athlete—a drop of orange juice formed and dripped onto the floor. As the cheers subsided, the athlete beckoned the man to come forward, asked his name, and then invited him to tell the crowd how he had managed to develop such fistic powers. "Nothing to it," replied the man; and then, with a grin, he added, "I happen to be the treasurer of the local Nazarene church."

An infant is born with a clenched fist; a man dies with an open hand. Life has a way of prying free the things that we think are so important.

"I'm a walking economy," a man was overheard to say. "My hairline's in recession, my waist is a victim of inflation, and together they are putting me into a deep depression."

Milton Segal

God loves a cheerful giver, but hates a grouch!

Melvin Maxwell

The bride, bent with age, leaned over her cane.
Her steps uncertain needed guiding. While
down the church aisle with a warm, toothless
smile, the groom in wheelchair gliding. And
who is this elderly couple thus wed? You'll
find when you closely explore it, that this is
that rare, most conservative pair who waited
until they could afford it.

Jack Taylor

❦ Don't give 'til it hurts.
　　Give 'til it feels good!

❦ Honk if you tithe!

Mark Hollingsworth

❦ God owns the cattle on a thousand hills and all the "taters" in those hills!

Uncle "Buddy" Robinson

One creative pastor was determined to have a record-breaking missions offering. He wired his pews to electrical currents and placed a buzzer on the pulpit. On Sunday at offering time, he asked, "How many will stand and pledge $100 to world missions offering?" He then pressed the buzzer giving everyone an electrical shock! Dozens stood immediately! He reported that his congregation gave a record-breaking offering—but to his dismay, several deacons were electrocuted!

❦ (From his pulpit . . .)

You ungrateful beasts, you are not worthy of the treasures of the Gospel. If you don't improve, I will stop preaching rather than cast pearls before swine.

Martin Luther

❦ He who gives when he is asked has waited too long.

Years ago, a little boy had two quarters—one for ice cream and one for the church offering.

Unfortunately, he accidentally dropped one into the storm sewer.

"Well, Lord," the boy said, "there goes your quarter!"

STEWARDSHIP SCRIPTURES

*Meditations and verses
to use before
the offering*

The earth is the LORD'S, and everything in it, the world, and all who live in it.

Ps. 24:1

For every animal of the forest is mine, and the cattle on a thousand hills.

Ps. 50:10

❧ Honor the LORD with your wealth, with the firstfruits of all your crops; then your barns will be filled to overflowing, and your vats will brim over with new wine.

Prov. 3:9-10

❦ And my God will meet all your needs according to his glorious riches in Christ Jesus.

Phil. 4:19

From everyone who has been given much, much will be demanded; and from the one who has been entrusted with much, much more will be asked.

Luke 12:48

♫ Give, and it will be given to you. A good measure, pressed down, shaken together and running over, will be poured into your lap. For with the measure you use, it will be measured to you.

Luke 6:38

He was in the world, and though the world was made through him, the world did not recognize him. He came to that which was his own, but his own did not receive him. Yet to all who received him, to those who believed in his name, he gave the right to become children of God.

John 1:10-12

If anyone does not provide for his relatives, and especially for his immediate family, he has denied the faith and is worse than an unbeliever.

1 Tim. 5:8

❀ Remember this: Whoever sows sparingly will also reap sparingly, and whoever sows generously will also reap generously.

2 Cor. 9:6

❧ Happiness lies more in giving than in receiving.

Acts 20:35, NEB

When we give . . . we celebrate the gifts of God's love, hope, and encouragement.

When we give . . . we offer thanks to the One who gave the ultimate sacrificial gift.

When we give . . . we provide for the local church needs both today and for future generations.

There was a man, though some did count him mad, the more he cast away, the more he had.

John Bunyan

To give my life for Christ appears glorious . . . to pour myself out for others . . . to pay the ultimate price for martyrdom . . . I'll do it. I'm ready to go out in a blaze of glory.

Fred Craddock

❦ Our bodies, our minds, our spirits are all created by God. Our talents, gifts, and abilities are given to us by God.

We cannot do what God does and God will not do what we can do!

The fiscal health of the church will rise and fall with what we do—you and I! Stewardship is a lifestyle!

❀ Jesus Christ is the supreme example of giving living. Such generosity "demands my soul, my life, my all!"

Tithing is not a matter of money, it is an issue of trust.

John Maxwell

God is the owner and giver of all, we are His stewards.

C. Neil Strait

Generous giving produces rejoicing in one's soul.

David M. Vaughn

Giving to God should be a time of worship, rejoicing, and celebration. Giving is our grateful response to God for all things.

Giving should not be done
because of pressure,
it should be done through praise
and pleasure.

Each week we bring our tithes and offerings. They have been lovingly set aside to further the work of the kingdom of God.

❦ The work of God is not accomplished by a few tithers. It requires many faithful stewards doing their best.

I want to tell you something from observation.

I have never met anyone who tithed who did not tend to be happy about the fact he did. He was not just happy about tithing . . . but about a lot of other things.

I've never met anybody who tithed very long, who gave it up.

I have never met anyone who tithed who did not say at some time it has been extremely difficult . . .

Generous people seem to be the happy ones. Miserly people seem to be the unhappy ones. The critical spirit is with those who are not giving people. Just look around you and you can tell.

Ben Haden

STEWARDSHIP SOLUTIONS

Questions and answers on biblical stewardship

Question: Who should give?

Answer: "Each one of you should set aside a sum of money in keeping with his income" (1 Cor. 16:2).

Question: When should we give?

Answer: "On the first day of every week"
(1 Cor. 16:2).

Question: Where should we give?

Answer: "'Bring the whole tithe into the storehouse, that there may be food in my house. Test me in this,' says the LORD Almighty, 'and see if I will not throw open the floodgates of heaven and pour out so much blessing that you will not have room enough for it'" (Mal. 3:10).

Question: How much should we give?

Answer: "For if the willingness is there, the gift is acceptable according to what one has, not according to what he does not have" (2 Cor. 8:12).

Question: Why should we give?

Answer: 1. to support the ministers of God and His church (Phil. 4:15-16)

2. to evangelize the world (Heb. 13:16)

Question: How can I be a happy giver?

Answer: "Each man should give what he has decided in his heart to give, not reluctantly or under compulsion, for God loves a cheerful giver" (2 Cor. 9:7).

Question: Did Jesus discuss giving?

Answer: "Do not store up for yourselves treasures on earth, where moth and rust destroy, and where thieves break in and steal. But store up for yourselves treasures in heaven, where moth and rust do not destroy, and where thieves do not break in and steal. For where your treasure is, there your heart will be also" (Matt. 6:19-21).

Question: Do I really have to give 10 percent?

Answer: "And Abraham gave him a tenth of everything" (Heb. 7:2).

Question: Will I experience blessings when I give?

Answer: "And God is able to make all grace abound to you, so that in all things at all times, having all that you need, you will abound in every good work" (2 Cor. 9:8).

Question: How can I acknowledge the lordship of Christ?

Answer: "But seek first his kingdom and his righteousness, and all these things will be given to you as well" (Matt. 6:33).

Question: What is the ultimate gift given in Scripture?

Answer: "For God so loved the world that he gave his one and only Son, that whoever believes in him shall not perish but have eternal life" (John 3:16).

WHY I TITHE

With my tithe I seal a bargain, With my tithe I pay a debt.
With my tithe I serve a purpose That my God will not forget.
With my tithe I fish for sinners, With my tithe I find the lost.
With my tithe I gird the winners, With my tithe I share the cost.
With my tithe I love my neighbor, With my tithe I pass a test.
With my tithe I clothe His image In a form one-tenth divine.
With my tithe I build a temple, With my tithe I feed its fire.
With my tithe I still a yearning Of my soul's innate desire.
With my tithe I heal the stricken, With my tithe they rise again.
With my tithe I walk with giants, In the wake of Godly men.
With my tithe I walk in honor Where the great and strong have trod.
With my tithe I store my treasures In the treasure house of God!

Peter E. Long

Stan Toler serves as pastor-in-residence at Southern Nazarene University in Bethany, Oklahoma. Stan has given his life to seeing the kingdom of God grow with power and grace. He is known as a pastor-to-pastors and is a gifted leader, administrator, and inspirational speaker.

Stan has pastored three of the fastest-growing churches in the United States, including Heritage Memorial Church (Ohio), Oklahoma City First, and Nashville First Nazarene churches.

Never content with the status quo, Stan has also traveled around the world, helping churches and organizations in evangelism, leadership, and stewardship. He is also a popular speaker.

Since 1972, when Stan and the founder of INJOY Ministries, John Maxwell, developed their first stewardship campaign, Stan has been conducting stewardship month emphases in the local church.

Stan has dedicated himself to writing, having now written a dozen books and manuals on what he knows best: church management, evangelism, stewardship, and helps for pastors.

Additional copies of this book can be ordered (number 083-411-6553) from:

Beacon Hill Press of Kansas City
P.O. Box 419527
Kansas City, MO 64141
(1-800-877-0700)